FLESH

Winner of the 1998 Marianne Moore Poetry Prize

*The Marianne Moore Poetry Prize
was established in 1991 by Helicon Nine Editions,
and is awarded annually to a previously unpublished
manuscript chosen by a distinguished writer
through an open nationwide competition.*

The judge for 1998 was Robert Phillips.

FLESH

POEMS
Susan Gubernat

Winner of the
1998 Marianne Moore Poetry Prize

Selected by Robert Phillips

HELICON NINE EDITIONS
KANSAS CITY AND LOS ANGELES

© 1999 by Susan Gubernat

All rights reserved under International and Pan American Copyright Conventions.
Published by Helicon Nine Editions, a division of
Midwest Center for the Literary Arts, Inc.
P. O. Box 22412, Kansas City, MO 64113
www.heliconnine.com
Requests to copy any part of this work should be addressed to the publisher.

Grateful acknowledgment is made to the editors of the following magazines and anthologies in which these poems first appeared, sometimes in slightly different versions: *Nantucket Review, Sojourner, 100 Words, The Nassau Review, Whose Woods These Are* (WordWorks; "To The Close Friend Most Unlike Me" won the 1982 WordWorks Washington Prize), *Womanblood: Portraits of Women in Poetry and Prose* (Continuing Saga Press).

I would like to thank the New Jersey Council on the Arts for a grant that helped me begin work on this book and Nassau Community College for a sabbatical that enabled me to complete it.
Special thanks to Molly Peacock, mentor extraordinaire.

Cover and book design: Tim Barnhart
Cover illustration: *In the Sauna* by Beth Krommes. Wood engraving

Helicon Nine Editions is funded in part by the National Endowment for the Arts, a federal agency, and by the Kansas Arts Commission and the Missouri Arts Council, state agencies.

Library of Congress Cataloging-in-Publication Data

Gubernat, Susan
    Flesh : poems / Susan Gubernat.-- 1st ed.
      p. cm.
    ISBN 1-884235-28-X (acid-free paper)
    1. Working class--United States--Poetry. 2. Immigrants--United States--Poetry. 3. Catholics--United States--Poetry. I. Title

PS3557.U234 F58 1999
811'.54 21--dc21

                                                                                    99-040051

Manufactured in the United States of America
FIRST EDITION
HELICON NINE EDITIONS
KANSAS CITY AND LOS ANGELES

In memory of my grandmother Helen

"This hunger for sound is almost as sharp as desire, as if one could honour every inch of flesh in words; and so, suspend time."
—Anne Michaels, *Fugitive Pieces*

CONTENTS

I.

- 11   Working Class
- 12   Belles Lettres
- 13   Nutcracker
- 15   The Nuns
- 17   First Haircut
- 18   Pomegranate Season
- 19   Les Oncles
- 21   Parish
- 23   My Father's Cornet
- 24   To Sedna, the Inuit Sea Goddess
- 25   Fontanelle
- 26   Flesh
- 27   The Midwife
- 28   To the Close Friend Most Unlike Me
- 29   My Parents Buy a Burial Plot
- 30   Death's Details
- 31   Here's a Christmas Card

II.

- 35   The First Night of Fireflies
- 36   Wild Girls
- 37   Women and Men: A Retrospective
- 38   Corporal Works of Mercy

39	Splitting Wood
40	Ambergris
42	Lot's Wife
43	Winter Solstice
44	Flu Season
45	Cherry-ripe
46	Ruined Statues in the Louvre
47	Cana
49	November
50	The Man Who Touched the Twelve-Armed Goddess
52	Epithalamion

III.

55	Literally
56	Reading James Wright
57	Leda's Children
58	To Become an Islander
59	Flowering Cherry and Autumn Maple with Poem Slips
61	Composing on the Computer
62	Teacher to a Mad Student
65	Boomers
66	Caution Horses
67	*Biographical Note*

I.

Working Class

How often in my presence someone's used
that term and I find myself being discussed
in the third person, everyone in my family
maligned as an illiterate subtext. The foundry
where my grandfather worked, where he held
in his head formulas the chemists had forgotten,
would have made him foreman if only he'd learned
to write in English. He was too proud to stumble
in public, through years of night classes declining
verbs, tight-rope walking the faint blue lines
of a student's notebook. Once he'd swung
out on the cantilevered bridge he crossed to work
every day, wild, hatless, to impress the woman
who became my grandmother. He risked falling
into the dirty industrial river to cry out "I am"
just as, later, he drove his cars recklessly
through all intersections, leaning on his horn
and shouting, in Polish, "Get out of the way. I am coming."
And he was. And they were. And we have been.

Belles Lettres

She had learned
to sip tea from a glass,
hot, round-lipped and cloudy,
without slurping,
to disguise her wide forehead,
wrapped in a silk scarf
the color of lapis, of peacock feathers.

She had made her voice round.

In the country she was thought a city woman,
in the city, taken for pastoral,

and so was exotic everywhere.

She told her poverty like a story
to people who thought it beautiful
and asked for more in small quantities

all the while conjuring for herself
the stink of cabbage in her family's hallway—

they'd called it a "vestibule,"
which made her love words.

Nutcracker

Not to be confused with the little wooden priapus
that waltzed a sleepy girl across the room,
nor with the dance itself, although you could
make some connections—the fanged quality
of the gift with this, my story. And then
there's the holiday supper in both, too: warm
flannel nightgowns and weird adults
hanging around, like the cousin-once-removed,
burned to death in her bed smoking cigarettes
alone, nodding over movie magazines.
She watched us say our prayers together
every Christmas Eve. Or my father's so-called
bachelor uncle whose favorite present
was the fifth he cradled in the crook
of his arm like old Joseph in a crèche
and carried safely back to his room
in a rooming house in the worst part
of town. These and others all would gather
at my grandmother's between the moment Venus
blinked and midnight mass. But where was *she?*
Even when the plate piled high with
pecans, almonds, chestnuts, and Brazil nuts
arrived, and the cracking began, a chorus of knuckle
bones, shells scuttling across the tablecloth,
deep digging for the walnuts' meat, a last dessert,
she was nowhere to be seen. My grandfather's
nutcracker. I'd found her one day, I guess
by accident, cached in a velvet-lined drawer
of the china server with fancy matches
and the flamingo-shaped cocktail stirrers
we sometimes played with. She was half a woman
—from the waist down—smooth, dark, and wooden,
etched with buttocks and a belly button, and hinged

so that her legs spread wide open and right
below her crotch (they said to call it that as if trees
themselves were virginal) each thigh was notched
deep enough to hold a whole nut still, for cracking.
Yet they never used her, as far as I saw.
Never did my kindly grandfather, who blushed
at all obscenity and once, they say, confessed
to a priest about his lust rising as he watched
a movie orgy on TV, reach into the drawer
where I knew he kept her. I took her out,
secretly. I clicked her empty legs like castanets.

The Nuns

When our nun drove the idiot's head into the blackboard
it went so far, it went to the other side of God.
We watched her do it, too little to stop her,
mute as tiny, glass-eyed foxes around the necks
of the women at Mass who were thinking
of the piss stains their old men had left on the sheets
for them this morning and not of the wafer
raised aloft, like a third Ace in poker.
This boy was stupid, he couldn't do something—
five times nine or the capital of Peru. 45. Lima.
Oh God, why don't you give him the answer?
I knew the answers. They'd never hurt me.

Besides, I loved the glimpse of linens on their supper
table, the glass goblets for water. I loved the chime
of the convent bell ringing against the waxed
corridors, the way someone had gone down
on her knees to make tiles into mirrors,
and the fact that they dressed without any.
How deftly, with straight black pins, they kept
their habits together. If I bent down, retrieved
a pin shaken loose from the layers of black gauze—
the wedding-portrait's negative—she smiled at me
and pinned a layer closer to her breast.

And the boy, he was shaking and crying when she cuffed
him again—this time, for shaking and crying. He cradled
his head in his arm, loped back to his desk
near the windows where lilacs other girls brought
from their paltry gardens surrounded a shrine
to Mary, if it was May. Our roses were always so slow
I could bring them only at month's end
when we stopped having processions and started

exams. Overnight, they blew from buds into faces,
displayed their grizzled yellow cores. Then
it was summer, and the boy heaved rocks
at the smaller ones who passed his vacant lot,
the boy rode his bicycle over the legs of a little girl

playing alone in the alley. Years later, in the grip
of a lover, I walked onto the forbidden beach
at Cape May where it's said the nuns spend
their summers, where they lift off the starched
wimple cutting so deeply into their brows,
where they reveal their arms and their legs to each other.
And because it was winter, the wide porch
was silent, the long skirts of the wind swept
the floorboards, rocking chairs upended and stacked.

That night, I kept coming—his one finger, a miracle.
I wouldn't stop, not even when the maid rapped
at the door softly, then harder, to remind us of check-out.
Not even from thirst, or from hunger.

First Hair Cut

The barber's rough bristles brushed
up my nape, swept shoulders,
clavicle, breastbone under the drape.
He laid the horsehair beside
the stinging colognes, the combs
plunged into a murky bath,
and untied me, flapped the cover once,
folded it like a flag.
He spun me back to the mirror,
thrust the looking-glass into my hand —
with a courtier's sly indignity,
a pride in this craft,
in what his scissors had whistled
around my ears, the razor had hummed:
Empty, mädchen. Empty.
You won't find Medusa in there.
I looked down.
Wet hair coiled on the old linoleum.
The fluorescent light licked
my bare neck to stone.

Pomegranate Season

First frost—the sugar-shocked leaves
crunched beneath our metal skates. We bought
pomegranates nestled in blue tissue, crates
of them beside the pickle barrel, rows
of ugly red ornaments, stem ends frayed
as if they'd been wrenched from their trees.
It took a sharp knife to split them
down the center so we could dig beneath
the milky fontanelle for the garnet seed clusters,
hard, sour nipples that made our mouths
pucker, juices rolling down our fingers
and into our sleeves. It was the season
of a cellar door slamming, vampire
darkness—God, I'd barter my soul for these.

Les Oncles

"Snow on the roof but fire in the cellar"
the uncles used to say, to shame us at Christmas,
like speaking a foreign tongue.
The aunts would scold
and clear away cups from the white dinner cloth.

I knew there must be something dark,
deep-down and hot about it for old men,
something they stoked like a coal fire
on a rough night in March
when wind curled at the backs of their necks
on pillows next to their wives,

something they took out like a war prize
in front of the godchildren,
a dagger or luger
snatched back when little girls
went to touch it,
put away in the leather box
full of handkerchiefs

with the pictures of French girls
eating chocolates and smiling
on one of those bridges over the Seine.
Those were the days they learned
the routes to a girl's heart—gifts of
sheer nylon stockings, the kind
women gave up back home,
like chocolate, to help win a war.

Voulez-vous coucher avec moi?
is all the French the uncles remember.
For years it was safe to tease us about it

until my first Christmas in flesh-colored stockings.
I had learned enough of that language to ask
"But didn't you use the familiar?"

Parish

The priests, the priests
in their loneliness imagined our lives
but thinly.
They pulled chasubles over their heads
and imagined our lovemaking—
wooden boats brushing up against the pier
at night, the heave, the haw of tides
straining the knot, the lifting
above the tideline, easing into berth,
the letting go
the holy salt on their tongues, oh God.

The priests ate milky suppers alone,
their housekeeper's broad-backed floral apron
always in retreat.
At dusk, candles back in place on the sideboard,
dishes stacked, drying,
the priests imagined our evenings—
baby crawling toward the hot stove,
girl's crayon scrawl all over the pantry,
blue rim of milk left in the little boy's glass.

In noon sun flashing like a chalice
they drove to our deathbeds.
And imagined our deaths—
souls rising like helium balloons to the ceiling,
children's screams bouncing against hallways,
doors slamming, the drone of the TV, *oh pray for us*.
What miracles did we have to offer them?

At christenings, the priests sniffed the godmothers'
perfumes, imagining incest and sodomy.
They watched us play baseball at picnics,
tasting blood, tasting cinder grit in the hollows of our knees.

They imagined our sins differently.
We told the same ones over and over
until they could write sermons about them,

our lackluster sins, our commonness.
The priests illuminated every lie, every grudge,
every knife fight until it glowed like Moses.

When they pressed the host to our tongues
—*This is my body*—
they imagined our Amen, Amen, Amen
to mean yes, we carry you forth into the world,
we bear you into the world,
the gods that you are,
the men you imagine yourselves to be.

My Father's Cornet

The parched leather case, flecked in the corners,
stored cold up the polished stairway no one climbed,
crackled like an old snake's molting. Its latches sprung
open with a sour twang, its felt and velvet lining,
crushed purple of vestments, sent up the oldest smell
I knew, older than book binding—moth pages
falling to the floor in little heaps—older, it seemed,
than the tool room in the cellar, where grandpa's
straw boater, the one he never wore, hung on a peg.
If we got that far, he'd let us palpate the valve buttons,
milky mother-of-pearl caps clicking, drumming
of stunted fingernails, run our hands along the slide,
screw the silver mouthpiece into the pipe and blow.

My father rarely played for us. He lost, he said, his lip
sometime after the war. He must mean, I thought,
the upper one, which, next to Satchmo's, struck
me as thin and weak. A nickel-colored, dented mute
nestled in the case, and when he played he stuffed
it in so that the baby wouldn't wake. There always was
a baby. You don't live that life, don't go on the road
with a new family, and besides, the drugs, the booze
were not for him. He'd seen enough. No more sleeping
on a beach. No more solos. No more reveille.
He wiped spit from its mouth, took it apart, piece by piece.
It disappeared for years, along with his little spoils
of war: the luger and the sword we knew he stole
from an officer, some Nazi he'd gotten that close
to. We never learned much more.

To Sedna, the Inuit Sea Goddess

In the storm when your father flung
you out of his boat into the grey sea
and when he hacked off your fingers as you clung
to the rocking sides, wondering if he were crazy,

did you think: "His will to live
is greater than my life." And you slipped
like stone beneath the wave
while the little fingers ripped

from knuckle bone floated, then dove,
after you, becoming sharks, whales, seals,
your retinue, your playmates, all the love
left for a fishy girl who breaks fishermen's reels

in season, blows up storms to send their boats
to the bottom. Do you know your father wept
for you once the sun rose?
And that he killed himself?

Or do your new fins speed you from your cave
toward every wreck that settles near your home
hoping that this time your bitter wave
has brought your father, and all his work, down.

Fontanelle

The soul keeps pouring in before it closes.
I sit at the crater's edge and wish
for rain, more rain, rain enough to fill
this tender patch, this hollow. *Don't drop*

the baby. Soft spot. Fragrance of voyages.
Membrane, not a flapping kite or sail.
Outside, the cranky wind fumbles
for keys. In here, the taste of sleep.

Meanwhile you're knitting, cell by cell,
a carapace to meet the world—a helmet's
what you'll need, a bunker. Something
the doctor will approve, as doctors will.

Kilauea blows its ancient seal.
Skylights open in the earth
and they reveal deep liquid fire
running red beneath the crust

and lava flows that knot up
like a baby's fists. I kiss you there—
more gently here on top,
before the small skull shuts.

Flesh

for Max

Your newborn neck recalls the potter's fragrant spit,
sweet dust of the workroom before the firing,
salmon tinge of clay before the feast.
You were a vessel thrown on the wheel
where fingers worked your ribs, lip, feet
and thumbs pressed deep to sculpt the sockets
holding grandma's eyes, brought back from the treasure-house,
just as mad and milky dim as when we buried them.

The Midwife

fingers a pelvis model
thrust on a stick like sculpture
makes a fist to show
how the baby crowns
she loves those bones
and their unknitting
the way they separate like continents

she has the mother cradle
the head emerging
look, as her fist does now,
plunged through the model
she will get behind the woman
on all fours
as in the Kama Sutra
to ease the birth

she rocks her small body
swivels her narrow hips
as she talks to you
about easing the impossible passage
ah with sound
ooh ah with touch

at the kitchen table
her son, with the wide forehead and crossed eyes,
clatters his trucks, like anybody's son

To the Close Friend Most Unlike Me

Sunday, I thought of you—
driving over unfamiliar roads, I nearly killed
two little boys who cut across my path on those infernal,
low-slung, carnival-colored bicycles,
wheels wobbling out of control.
From the safe curbside, they made faces at me.
Nearly killed them, and the little girl who,
that morning, overheated, sprung free from services,
had dashed across the road without a glance.
How her father will beat her, I thought, as I sped up,
watching him grab and shake her into cold sanity in his terror.
I thought of us, really, running from our mugs of tea
and limpid conversation in your kitchen
at the sound of rubber thumping over plastic,
screeching to a stop.
We watched with mouths hanging open like wells
as the car reversed, then revealed
the intaglio of child stamped into pavement.
The riderless bike, pinwheeling down the block,
stubbed its front tire at the curb and stopped.
How you broke from my side, you the minister's renegade daughter,
to hold the boy's mother as they draped him in grey,
then poured stinging whiskey down her throat—rites of consolation,
still deep in your bones, invoked. While I swallowed dry,
and shook with the feckless passion to slap someone—
the little boy under the wheel of that car, for instance—alive.

My Parents Buy a Burial Plot

It took her fifteen years to get him
to buy her a house—fifteen years of spring Sundays riding
around neighborhoods, nauseated in the backseat,
to look at homes we'd never own.
It's taken only ten for this: a double-decker
in Heaven's Gate, East Hanover. They are well,
on her birthday eat lobster, drive winding country
roads far afield from the little coffin of a house where we were raised.
They put their money down.

I hate the spring. We'd leave the city regularly
to romp in the cemetery near grandma's headstone,
Jesus sculpted in high relief, marble cheekbones,
hardy geraniums. "Not a day goes by," my mother says,
"that I don't think of her." So I'm a piss-poor daughter:
that's a claim I could never make.

Anyway, it houses four to six. We could all
be together again. She suspects her little agnostics
prefer burning to decay, the furnace's roar
to the worms' sighing. Still, she lets me know
there's space for me, the way the slab of bed
in the Raggedy Ann room of her house still waits,
clean sheets stretched tight, end to end, for my single, guiltless body.

She knows I could never be buried in sacred ground
nor rise up, whole and perfect, on the final harrowing
from the hole in East Hanover, jam-packed as I am
with the seven deadlies. She'll turn around to check
the backseat where we've been napping, and I'll be gone.
I'll be in hell if she's been right all along.

Death's Details

She irons her mother's dress for the open casket
the mourners will file past tomorrow   the way we look at rooms
in historic houses   we keep the coins in our pockets quiet,
cheek to cheek, those dead profiles, trusting

But where is He now, the one we crane our necks to see?
Riding on the parade float—flowers, thousands of bare
arms waving   we turn from the wall, we are steamy
with hope, we expect to see Him at last, upright

in that metal chair drawn into the bed curtain's circle,
hospital holy of holies   but it's no one,
or worse, another human: the nurse's hands that pleat
and fold   they make packages of everything

And those stories—the wise ones were good
housekeepers, filling and trimming their lamps while
the foolish danced their slippers to bits in a subterranean
mead hall   burn His cheek with the tallow of desire

and you'll never see Him   how the iron's sweep
flattens out the puckers around the neck,   the cloth hot
for a moment, almost seared   and then relaxing
into the shape of the neat collar she'll wear into the ground

Here's a Christmas Card

with the blank look of Abbot Thayer's angel
    hollow, not holy, stunned —
    the god just ran off with a pagan
though he left her these wings

she'll rise above the rutting
    earth into the marrow of the sky
    after all, how can she abide
seasons men keep like maps on a napkin

tracing sun and moon, the most awkward
    of all their inventions
    look how they measure
the moon's pale cuticle as if

the moon were ever blood-
    less, as if web and nest
    originated here on earth
and not in the bright throbbing of the stars

II

The First Night of Fireflies

It would be this way: twilight
a thin net over the garden, her roses
and her roses' thorns. My grandmother,
creaking on the landing, faced
the door, its window, yellow shade drawn.
Some boy already had a glass jar
with a grass nest, a punctured lid.
He was coming over.

Wild Girls

Wild girls are all around us
and the memory of snow

They clutch at each other
then go south for the winter

What marks their faces?
Geese trundle away

Their eyes—gills flashing,
cold spawning upstream

Hearts like winterberries
crack, crack of a rifle

They have no opinions
falls the silver barometer

They are full of opinions
falls the moon into river

Wild girls are singing
Foxhair caught in a bramble

Wild girls are dancing
Bears groan in the forest

Women and Men: A Retrospective

> *"I paint odalisques in order to paint the nude.... Otherwise, how is the nude to be painted without being artificial? But also, I know they exist. I was in Morocco. I saw them."*
>
> —Matisse

I know they exist, I saw them —
women and men who live their whole
lives together. She was my grandmother
who fattened into a great china bowl,
the kind bread rises in under a damp cloth.
He was a spring twig sprouting. He wound
the cuckoo clock by dragging the weights
down every night until that time
he foamed at the mouth. "My man,"
she claimed, and bathed him.
Who knew their rocking bodies,
shallow with sleep, under the shadow
of the plaster virgin, who knew
what great delight, what sorrow
each had passed on to the other?
The cellar lamp left on all night,
the coal bins empty. "Speak to me of love"
urged the translation in the rouged
voice of the torch singer. I can't.
I saw these two in another place
among the merchants, the fruitsellers,
bearing burdens on their backs,
walking uphill, fully clothed.

Corporal Works of Mercy

Can there be passion in a house
where each feeds the other,
where I hold your head in my lap
or you hold mine?

We repair each other
bit by bit like old china.

You came off the road to live here.
I, stuck like a tack in this landscape,
wanted brethren, yes but more:
mouth at my mouth, at my thigh.

We set down plates for one another,
share our nakedness like bread,
then cover it.

I offer myself in dreams
to every passing stranger
or dream that you do.

Still, the table is laid each evening.
One calls out into the fields
                      the other comes.

Splitting Wood

It's best when you take off your shirt

and swing   and backbone extends into arm

arm into ax   ax into blade.

Into the log heart.

I watch from a corner of the yard

where I'm weeding. Midsummer.

And freeze you at the height of a swing

shut my eyes   wait for the fall

in darkness   for the "tock"

as it strikes well, saying,

winter, this will burn between us.

Ambergris

> *John and Lydia*
> *That lovely pair*
> *A whale killed him*
> *Her body lies here*
> —epitaph in a cemetery on Martha's Vineyard

Caught in the cobblestones, her heel
broke off and she thought
of him riding the whale
as he rode her into the trough
of the unmade bed the day,
distracted, she had filled
all the lamps too full,
spilled the musky oil
across his maps; it soaked
clear through the Galapagos,
streamed down the continent's
leeward side to the Cape
when she knew she was afraid
the child, leaping
inside her like dolphins
now, would perish.

The peas were blooming,
pretty faces strung
on the garden rigging,
strawberries soon to come,
tight white hearts.
She'd salt the slugs to save them.
Daylight lasted now so long
the full moon rose before

her time. She often missed
the first bold blink

of the evening star. Where
he was, was winter.

He didn't know about the child.
His last packet bore a nutmeg
stone she'd since grated down,
a tale of cook and his "poison"
soup, a painted fan,
and love for her, alone.
The scrimshawed fang
that hung between her breasts
—his last voyage's gift, carved
between Holmes Hole
and the Great Barrier Reef—
knocked, bone on bone.

Lot's Wife

The last time we cast shadows
on the wall
like wrestlers coiling

noon sun in the marketplace

but this was evening
I'd sent the servants out
kept the fire alive myself

So young, he had to be told
things

So young, he listened
as if I were a rabbi

Here, yes, and here, yes, and here

Have they escaped?
They were loading their shaky cart
when we hurried past

He trained his eyes on
the rim of his mother's shadow

I bury a laugh remembering
hair curling at the nape
the small lobe I hung an earring on

and God, his mouth, his wet mouth,
always the taste of

Winter Solstice

Our new pup backs into her plastic den.
No struggle: food's the lure, and a plaything
she can grind and worry. No whimpering
behind her stainless bars, not even when

I dim the ceiling lights, welcome dark noon
into the quiet house. I fear nothing
more than this—wildness sleeping
in the middle of a day rain

freezes as it leaves the sky, as we speak
its name. "Rain," an Irish Wolfhound in another
life of mine, a name I heard just once

called out by a young man at the peak
of a hill, fur streaming like sweat in the summer
as she leapt straight for him into the sun.

Flu Season

We keep passing the fever between us, a monster's
hot eye, milky taste of our deaths.
You predicted a dusting of snow. Now roofs
at the seacoast split their laps open and it comes,
quietly. We keep to our own beds, opposite
sides of the island, and pound, and pound.
Last night I thought: I'll wring out a cold
cloth for the top of the banister, the desk lamp,
whatever I find in the shape of your forehead,
pour warm tea into flowerpots, read
fabliaux to the blue digits on the clockface
until I roil into sleep, miles from you, love,
while you are spiking, soaked in your own sweat.

Cherry-ripe

Here you are again, on that shaky ladder in the south
of France, pulling off fistfuls of cherries, mahogany-
dark as my parents' dresser where I once carved (oh agony
to them) my name in wavy script, pouting
over the new baby. However did that puppet mouth
of yours, that tightened seam, turn pulpy, lush as any
splattered fruit? By dusk, the orchard ground grew rainy
with the cherries' blood. My time was running out.
Call it a working honeymoon, though this was play,
this harvest, helping a couple we barely knew
bundle their fruit into mesh bags before it got rotten.
A diversion. They thanked us both for saving the day
before we took off for the lonely room where you
chose one more night without love and left me barren.

Ruined Statues in the Louvre

Infant Love left his palm print on this Aphrodite's naked back.
(Aphrodite crouches armless. Her head is gone.)
Love's fingers, fossilized in bas
relief, are slightly spread, grazing her spine.
The child, sweating after wild play, stopped
against his mother near some riverbank or well—
that kind of cold. Her round rump low, propped
on an upturned heel, torso swayed but stable,
she let Love rest there lightly, his wild energy saved.
You don't remember this, I know: as we passed
all that bristling stone—stags' antlers, bearded slaves,
dismembered gods, Etruscan couples leaning fast
against each other in their tombs—for the hundredth time or so
that day, you let my hand go.

Cana

I walk the dog beside the Sound
at twilight. The pair of swans
that preen and float near shore
are nowhere to be found.
Two wedding guests in black
replace them—they're here to smoke
in plein air on the promenade.
They lean against the rail
and murmur, their backs to me
and to the onion-domed catering
hall across the street—the Sans Souci,
stirring like a birdhouse now,
the hour between the vow
and the festivities. A white stretch
limo prowls the street, windows
blackened, and inside, a row
of tiny lights, the kind that mark
a darkened theater's aisles
so latecomers can stumble
to their seats. Invisible
bride, invisible groom ride
in this hearse, in this cocoon.

My dog could pounce and slaver
on the wedding guests, so I restrain her.
Once, off-leash, she leapt into water
after seabirds mounting far
beyond her reach, and into a current
that nearly swept her away.
I could pounce, too, middle-aged

landlubber, eager to chatter
about the albatross of love.

But these two seem sufficient
-ly dour so I leave them to their nicotine,
and contemplation of the rusty barge
across the harbor and the dredging
machine on the opposite beach.

I think of Hamlet's petulant
"we will have no more marriage"—
that foolish adolescent's rant,
more toothless than Polonius,
and my own knee-jerk cant. When
the truth is the dressmaker's dummy
in the bridal shop each season
wears a new gown I measure mentally
against my collarbone
—though I swore off it all, I swear,
when I molted my satin wedding dress
like a mummy's rags
in a consignment store in the Midwest.

And there's that limo again
taking the s-curves of this road
as if they're right angles, its cargo
maybe as jostled and smeared up
as senior prom. Who knows? You'd
have to be that young to enjoy the ride.
Or drunk. Or better, both. Ah, the cynic
kicking in! and right on time,
as the dog, tacking like the sailboats
heading home against the wind,

takes a shit not far from where
the wedding guests have ground the ends
of cigarettes into the grass meridian
opposite the Sans Souci. A waiter
dims the chandelier for cocktail hour
just as the harbor waters turn to wine.

November

Here comes our last storm with thunder.
The leaves hang on. So does the morning moon,
chalk dust slapped against the sky, a rough
ghost kiss. I can't forget those fifty nobby lily bulbs
I drove into the ground, trailing old women's
whiskers, or the acid mix of peat and dirt I made
to hold them. I can't stir my own womb.
It's too late.

Here comes the wind that will shake down
the oak tree, what's left of it after June's gypsy
moths, their awful crunching and grinding.
They rappelled into the old rose on sticky
lines, and ate. The blooms grew weak,
each fainter until All Souls' Day, while juice
shot up the stems, filled to the brim those
fat rosehips.

Here comes the rain we needed all summer,
the nudging, pinprick rain to feed
the onion grass. Insistent, all of it,
about a winter crop. What do you call the dust
that forms on ornamental cabbages
poking their purple bums up under the snow?
And the dust that settles in the cleavage
of ripe plums?

The Man Who Touched
the Twelve-Armed Goddess

"I am clever, " says the man. "The guards
        never catch me."
Clever—such a milk face, sponge
        body, such a stifled cry
from the side of the glass case that houses
        tiny divinities he can never
touch: goddesses of flute, drum, lamp,
goddess of the exuberant dance.

He giggles at two women exposed,
        admonished for finger-tracing
the abduction of Sītā in high relief—
        Sītā, dangling half-naked
in the arms of Rāvana, pliant as rice leaf.

The women back off, and he advances.

He is glittering behind his glasses
        and flits from each to each—
a swipe at the rump of the elephant god,
        a nudge to a bodhisattva's knee.

How can I avoid him? his quick and dirty
        lectures on mythology,
his flicking tongue, his crumpled pants
        about to come undone.
All the stone maidens and their attendants,
        the boy perched on the temple bell,
long legs drawn up to his cleft chin. Omphalos
        of the Javanese prince, clay breast
of a languid nymph leaning against a capital.

Bronze nipples of the twelve-armed one

       he prizes, with the critics, above
the rest. "Unique," he says. "Perhaps
       a Cunda. A delicate Cunda. Quite unique."
He strokes her shoulder. All at once, it's over.
       He scurries to the next scene.
There is this god I remember, a young man really,
       cast in silver, nearly pure—floral loincloth,
curving ram's horns, necklace of claws, tiger teeth.

Epithalamion

The carpenters came.
Who invited

the carpenters?
The old lesbian—

her ox procession,
her orchestra.

They unpacked
levers and pullies,

winches shrieking
like seabirds.

They made the roof
rise for the bridegroom

of indeterminate size.
(My grandma says

you can tell by the toes.)
Those wacky carpenters

went out back for a smoke.
(They were union guys.)

On the altar the bride
stirred. It was the wind

that stirred her
and a black wing.

III

Literally

Abortion was merely a metaphor
for the nothing left in my life, the hollow
I had been trying my best to ignore

or fill up with politics and sex. A more
compelling choice didn't follow.
Abortion was only a metaphor

and that made it easy. Then I'd restore
myself to an original state and swallow
what I'd been trying my best to ignore:

the whirring machine, shudder at the core,
deep sucking, reversed. *Where does it go?*
Abortion was simply a metaphor

for real pain, maybe a little like labor.
I asked her: the nurse claimed she didn't know.
I have been trying my best to ignore

paradox in the word "aspirator,"
the work of unmaking. I need to show
how my abortion turned into a metaphor
I am now trying my best to ignore.

Reading James Wright

If I go down all the way with you
I won't come back up. That's the truth
of it. We mime Sappho but we are wingless,
the stumps of our shoulder blades
remind us we once had wings
that were torn from us.

I live near graves, and you know it's a posture.
I live near deer's tracks and admire
the pellets of scat, black fruit spilled
from a market basket. The town
has no center. It makes me dizzy

to think of plains stretched out
under a sky like this, flat blue, two coats,
pinned back by birds. The river's sloppy,
and the people all well and good.
Well. Good. I think they're stunned

by seepage. You'd say there's always
been something in the water.
There is nothing in the water, the old
woman assures me. When I come
roaring into the night, she burrows.

I'm alone here. You'd say we are always
alone. But I think you were lying.
Someone propped you up. Who
was it? Was it the boatman's lover,
lank and rambling? She never
threw herself into the sea.

Leda's Children

The swan honking of the woman
at the next table disgusts me—word
made flesh, or vice versa, as she spits
out some version of rancor toward
the invisible. I want to stare
in her direction so that the rest
recognize me for what I am: *not her*.
Still, this is ridiculous. My words
travel up and down my gullet,
my voice snarks through a reed
wet with mucus. I pick my way
carefully among the coils of green
shit she leaves behind, only to
step, once more, in my own.

To Become an Islander

Steal a sloop from the harbor
and go scalloping. Bloody
your hands with it.
Dive deep and give
your clothes a sea burial.
Return in rigging and sailcloth,
cunt stinging with brine.
Learn the laugh of the mad gull
and leave off mainland words,
idle glances at the ferry.
Now, in front of the mirror,
peel off the first layer
of old white skin —
burn your face brown before sunset.

Flowering Cherry and Autumn Maple with Poem Slips

(detail from a screen by Tosa Mitsuoki, c. 1654-7)

1

Poems pressed into your palm with your fare receipt.
Poems inspected by No. 53.
Poems stacked at the end of the trashman's pointy pole.
Poems on subscription cards falling out of magazines.
Poems stuck to the theater floor beneath your seat.
Poems the ticket taker rips in two.
   —Poems blowing like laundry from a tree

Papier-mâché poems glued back to back.
Flour-dusted poems buried in an old canister.
Tea-stained poems floating on a cracked saucer.
Crumb-laden poems sullen under the cake.
   —Poems blowing like laundry from a tree

Hard candy-button nipples pressed onto strips of poems.
Silver-foil, jagged-edged, spearmint wrappers backing poems.
Curved spill of vanilla slithering down cones onto poems.
Pale saltwater taffy tugging at the edges of poems.
Glazed apples-on-a-stick bibbed with thin layers of poems.
   —Poems blowing like laundry from a tree

Cantilevered work lamps dangling post-it poems.
Poems left in pink piles while you were away.
Mail slots silted with laser-printed poems.
Poems exchanged on cards with raised lettering.
Filofax poems jammed into the broken binding.
   —Poems blowing like laundry from a tree

Poems running along the bottom of your television screen.

Poems on the coaster lining your drink.
Poems left behind when tearing at the dotted line.
Poems pasted on the amber bottles of prescriptions.
Poems clipped and filed with family recipes.

2

Poems (the smell of mothballs, of cedar) pinned to wirehangers, last season's dry cleaning, at the back of the closet, unrecognizable, someone else's clothes, you don't remember that shrug of shoulder, hemline grazing the knee, where you wore it or for whom, what offending part of you it was meant to hide, what it was like to feel the garment from inside.

Composing on the Computer

I've learned to love the clicking of the keyboard —
small bones clattering against a neck,
at night, teeth grinding themselves down.
Trouble. Trouble. My nails keep growing.
Between the tiny rows, a bracelet unstrung,
dead fingertip cells wedge and rest.
If I could part the keys like doll's hair
the rosy scalp would spring up, fresh, alive.
Blind, I find my place on the hard, tiny nipples
of the letters "d" and "k"
     and when I want to move along, pump
the thin bar with the edge of my thumb,
leave nothing behind.
Tracks of bread in the forest for finding your way out,
a spool unwound.
Type: Tundra. Steppes. From the deep slot comes
the low, persistent growl they call a hum —
background noise now for every poem.

Teacher to a Mad Student

Your face is like an angel's.
I've kissed it
in my dreams.
I am therefore guilty.
Shattered angel,
surely it's celestial
to live on the edge
trumpeting out
beautiful madness
for I have told them
"I want you to find your own voices"
but what if one goes out
into the far fields for that
beyond the margins
to hear himself echo?
I have a desk where I sharpen
pencils, keep carbon copies.
This is the place I want you
to look into.
Mundane as a supermarket,
it's my life too.

2

"Come to Spain with me."

What do I say to that?
Like the first man who asked me
to marry him, it's tempting.

I married him.

I won't go to Spain with you.

3

In class I yak
about enjamb-
ment   caesura
while for you all things
are comingtogether
all things   suspending.

Then teacher turned traitor,
teacher turned magistrate
(same root)
I call them, thinking,
"Don't do this to me."
And they flank us, their
guns obvious as erections.

4

Before they take you
I try getting lost
but the cops get lost.
I steer them back
to the right room,
where I fed you coffee
("How do you take it?")
ironically, to calm you, myself.
You daze about Fair Oaks —
they'll take you there next.
You cough the word up like blood
to show me, oh this is real all right.
I know what you fear.

5

Near the elevator,
"Come with me."

I can't follow you down
nor lead you out of it
with sweet music.
If I look back
you'll vanish
like an old star.
I'll keep singing to myself.

   6

I wish you could have heard Ginsberg
last night, everyone singing Blake songs
"and all the hills ecchoéd,"
the children in us,
the madness made holy.
It's the nursemaid
who turns a blind eye to custom, to curfew,
spoils the little ones,
lets them stay out past sunset.
And it's too late now
but cover the fire, boy,
cover the fire.

Boomers

This is the last fallout shelter poem,
that phony genre. We never believed
in our own destruction. We were imbued
with the logic of eternity. And ready
for another diversion, something to
complain to our parents about. Admit it.
And stop making metaphors of the holocaust.
It didn't happen to us. That was that other
generation, remember? those we tried to shame
into building backyard bunkers
stocked with canned peas, bottled water, batteries
for radios to announce the all-clear
in a week or two. What were we thinking?
Secret clubhouses dug into the earth,
marathon checker games below spider
level, magical code rings, heroic comics
by flashlight. We would smuggle in a mail-order
chihuahua, tiny as a teacup, and feed her on leftovers.
Tinned spam, bars of brown soap, toilet
paper rolls—all would hold out. And we would emerge,
wearing Superman sunglasses, into the radiance of a new
dawn—with sharper angled shadows, perhaps—
turn on our televisions, slightly warm
to the touch, as if just switched off a moment ago,
and watch ourselves surfacing on one side
of the planet—lean, indestructible as those pale,
milky roots that are turned up under rocks,
clinging to half-lives, as we are now.

Caution Horses

hang their heads over the fence
and twitch their lips above their teeth
at the sight of the apple

hold out your hand to them
trembling
nod and speak about the sweetness
propped in your palm

the caution horses barely stretch
their vein-scored necks
to reach you—

across the field, below the rise,
invisible here,
branches heavy with fruit
sweep the ground

at their feet

Biographical Note

Susan Gubernat was born and raised in Newark, New Jersey. She has a graduate degree in English literature from Rutgers University and an MFA from the Iowa Writers' Workshop. A former magazine editor in New England and in the San Francisco Bay Area, she is an assistant professor in the English Department of Nassau Community College, Garden City, New York, where she specializes in Creative Writing, Women's Studies, and Journalism. She has been in residence at the Millay Colony and the MacDowell Colony. Her work has won the Washington Prize (WordWorks), a Woodrow Wilson Fellowship, and grants from the New Jersey Arts Council and New York Foundation for the Arts.

BOOKS BY HELICON NINE EDITIONS

FICTION

One Girl, a novel in stories by Sheila Kohler
Winner of the 1998 Willa Cather Fiction Prize, selected by William Gass

Climbing the God Tree, a novel in stories by Jaimee Wriston Colbert
Winner of the 1997 Willa Cather Fiction Prize, selected by Dawn Raffel

Eternal City, stories by Molly Shapiro
Winner of the 1996 Willa Cather Fiction Prize, selected by Hilary Masters

Knucklebones, 27 short stories by Annabel Thomas
Winner of the 1994 Willa Cather Fiction Prize, selected by Daniel Stern

Galaxy Girls:Wonder Women, stories by Anne Whitney Pierce
Winner of the 1993 Willa Cather Fiction Prize, selected by Carolyn Doty

Return to Sender, a novel by Ann Slegman

The Value of Kindness, short stories by Ellyn Bache
Winner of the 1992 Willa Cather Fiction Prize, selected by James Byron Hall

Italian Smoking Piece with Simultaneous Translation by Christy Sheffield-Sanford
A multi-dimensional tour de force

Sweet Angel Band, a first book of stories by R.M. Kinder
Winner of the 1991 Willa Cather Fiction Prize, selected by Robley Wilson

POETRY

Flesh by Susan Gubernat
Winner of the 1998 Marianne Moore Poetry Prize, selected by Robert Phillips

Diasporadic by Patty Seyburn.
Winner of the 1997 Marianne Moore Poetry Prize, selected by Molly Peacock

On Days Like This, poems by Dan Quisenberry

Prayers to the Other Life by Christopher Seid
Winner of the 1996 Marianne Moore Poetry Prize, selected by David Ray

A Strange Heart by Jane O. Wayne
Winner of the 1995 Marianne Moore Poetry Prize, selected by James Tate

Without Warning by Elizabeth Goldring
Co-published with BkMk Press, University of Missouri-Kansas City

Night Drawings by Marjorie Stelmach
Winner of the 1994 Marianne Moore Poetry Prize
Introduction by David Ignatow, judge

Wool Highways, poems of New Zealand by David Ray
Winner of the 1993 William Carlos Williams Poetry Award

My Journey Toward You, poems by Judy Longley
Winner of the 1993 Marianne Moore Poetry Prize
Introduction by Richard Howard, judge

Women in Cars, poems by Martha McFerren
Winner of the 1992 Marianne Moore Poetry Prize
Introduction by Colette Inez, judge

Hoofbeats on the Door by Regina deCormier
Introduction by Richard Howard

Black Method by Biff Russ
Winner of the 1991 Marianne Moore Poetry Prize
Introduction by Mona Van Duyn, judge

ANTHOLOGIES

Spud Songs: An Anthology of Potato Poems to benefit Hunger Relief
Edited by Gloria Vando and Robert Stewart

Poets at Large: 25 Poets in 25 Homes
Edited by H.L. Hix

The Helicon Nine Reader: A Celebration of Women in the Arts
Edited by Gloria Vando Hickok

FEUILLETS

Limited editions of little books, ranging in length from 4–24 pages

Ancient Musics, a poetry sequence by Albert Goldbarth
A Walk through the Human Heart, a poem by Robley Wilson
Christmas 1956, a poem by Keith Denniston
Climatron, a poem by Robert Stewart
Cortége, a poem by Carl Phillips
Down & In, poems by Dan Quisenberry
Dresden, a poem by Patricia Cleary Miller
Generations, a poem by George Wedge
The Heart, a short story by Catherine Browder
R. I. P., a poem by E. S. Miller
Short Prose, an illustrated essay by M. Kasper
Slivers, a poem by Philip Miller
Stravinsky's Dream, a story by Conger Beasley, Jr.
This is how they were placed for us, a poem by Luci Tapahonso
Tokens, a poem by Judy Ray